IF PRESSED

IF PRESSED

ANDREW MCEWAN

BOOKTHUG / 2017

ONTARIO ARTS COUNCIL
CONSEIL DES ARTS DE L'ONTARIO
an Ontario government agency
un organisme du gouvernement de l'Ontario

The production of this book was made possible through the generous assistance of the Canada Council for the Arts and the Ontario Arts Council. BookThug also acknowledges the support of the Government of Canada through the Canada Book Fund and the Government of Ontario through the Ontario Book Publishing Tax Credit and the Ontario Book Fund.

BookThug acknowledges the land on which it operates. For thousands of years it has been the traditional land of the Huron-Wendat, the Seneca, and most recently, the Mississaugas of the Credit River. Today, this meeting place is still the home to many Indigenous people from across Turtle Island, and we are grateful to have the opportunity to work on this land.

LIBRARY AND ARCHIVES CANADA CATALOGUING IN PUBLICATION

McEwan, Andrew, author
If pressed / Andrew McEwan. — First edition.

Poems.
Issued in print and electronic formats.
ISBN 978-1-77166-326-7 (SOFTCOVER)
ISBN 978-1-77166-327-4 (HTML)
ISBN 978-1-77166-328-1 (PDF)
ISBN 978-1-77166-329-8 (KINDLE)

I. Title.

PS8625.E93I3 2017   C811.6   C2017-905870-3
C2017-905871-1

Cover image: *Transverse Head-Tongue* (detail), 2013, by Lisa Nilsson
photography by John Polak

For those so misaffected.

Table of Contents

Of Matter Diverse and Confused. *Sect. 1.*

If Pressed. *Subsect. 1.*

And now we descend to particulars. Object capacity defines
name and difference. So briefly rest now, anatomized
body.

The desire to change performed in public. Or admirable
arts composed of excellent proportions. The heart and other
inferior parts.

We must agree that the disease is composed of the matter.
Function both depraved and repressed. Different writers imagine
sadness with humour or despair.

In the book the body putrefies. Most ardour cannot otherwise be. Omit
from the catalogue leaves placed in relief. We find our theories verified
in sleepers.

Frantic flesh. Certainty or distinction among so many casualties.
Cold, dry, and distemperature. Remember home. Macerate with cares.
Remember this perverse interior.

Vain Cures. *Subsect. 2.*

Balance passions and answers. The body is like a clock —
if one wheel is amiss, all the rest are disordered. The whole
fabric suffers.

Express doubt that politicians speak pure forms. Manias signify
those born to misaffected parents. Points to effects of imagination
and other maladies.

The awareness of a system acting upon the body, weighing
it down. On the other hand, an image to become acquainted with
as firm ground.

Bodily materials are either simple or mixed, vary according
to place. I'm devoted to a small room, a closed curtain. Adjust
the theoretical imbalance.

He is happy who can perform properly. Vain cures, no purpose.
Cause for punishment. Extricate from a labyrinth of doubts
and errors.

Victory was uncertain, acknowledging all of our offences. The conceit
alone troubles the craft of solitary living. We may never be
relieved of our diseases.

Cannot Face. *Subsect. 3.*

Affected atmospheres fog mirrored limbs. Movements figured
as dawning disallow rhetorical questions held as belief. Likewise
unapt objects.

We are no longer happy, but outside. Ascribe famous transformations
to the imagination: absurd, false, and violent. Public good
privileges the rest.

In this catalogue, you, our inseparable companion, symptom,
and chief cause. Tired with waking, and now slumbering
to continual task.

Poets and patients may go together for fabulous tales. Let them
be deluded. Fluid history flouts. Never to know what's coming next
and trouble bringing.

Those who speak strange languages likely fear death. They that
are all glass suffer no companionship. Infinite dangers trouble
business beforehand.

Afraid to voice in question. Not capable, docile. The fear of being
hanged. Hypochondriacs reclaim themselves in sickness. Sound
in an instant.

Depression Inventory

Check all that apply.

Sadness

earthquake ||
began || fissures || in
the US || I cannot stand
it || rumbled through
the || rest
of the world || sad
all the time || paroxysms
followed || sent
waves || sent
refugees || sent
speculation of || I
do not || feel
sad || collapse

1) caused or was caused by anxiety

2) caused or was caused by possibility of dislocation

3) caused or was caused by undermined growth

Pessimism

beware || anemia || currency
strategies || I do not expect things
to work out for me || prevent investment
it's a struggle I know as || leaders
stumble || feel hopeless || to quell
financial turmoil || contraction regionalizes
a body || lost || a body not
immune a || body
of deepening || disorder

1) quote crisis management

2) quote the EU

3) quote spillover in US dollars

Past Failure

I do not feel like a failure

||

welcome to the crisis economy

||

I have failed more than I should have

||

you could argue that we're culpable

||

as I look back I see a lot of failures

||

but we're not the ones posing risks at the moment

||

I am a total failure as a person

1) victim of optimism

2) victim of mercy

3) victim of natural forces

Loss of Pleasure

worst since || tense
great so now what || largest
since || last time || recent
weeks since || bail
outs || cut interest
rates since || nothing
feels good || to shoulder
this burden || under
stress || may cause
loss of appetite || may
result in loss || food
and energy || expected
to bounce || back

1) create feedback loop

2) create mounting pessimism

3) create ongoing inflation

Feeling Punished

regrettable downsides || fit the crime
I am being punished || sector regulation
by sector regulation || sometimes bad
things happen to good people || judge not lest
little expansion || punish me
bad people || mindful awareness
helps || a glutton for || good people
it hurts || reigned tightly || cursed to
dominate || working class interests
how to stop || punishing yourself
taken to extremes || bleed a little
I could be || a success
a martyr-preneur || but I am being
punished || regulated || held
in check || I always expected
punishment from || good people

1) list any changes since your last visit

2) list any independent agencies you have contacted

3) modify only one economic sector per question

Loss of Interest

stuck hard || an interest
in || consecutive
quarters || struggle
other people or || aging
economies || in the same mud
other people or objects || same
money || zero percent interest
in death spiral || now || firmly
below surface || other
people or activities || lost
comforts || reminders
defaults on a promise || I have
not lost || I have not
lost || it stuck || it didn't stay
with me || other people or
activities || without || loss
change of direction || all
things being equal || in
negotiation || or activities
a vested interest || other people
must stick it out

1) measurements less mild

2) not moderate or recognizable

3) at stake, negative or severe

Indecisiveness

seize opportunity || the decisive
moment || I used to self-report
decide to enact || inconsequential fixes
avoid fear and || expansion
must take further risks || trouble making
decisions for myself || scant rationale
present || expansion complicates
evenly || business as usual
avoidance mechanisms || but fortunate
sifting through wreckage || I trust
second guessing || scavengers
pick bones clean || opportunity
confuses || clarifies
wages threatened || decisions as
usual || more thinking not
better thinking || see opportunity
in a car crash || I think I make
decisions as well as || business
as usual

1) metaphors of weather

2) metaphors of mechanics

3) metaphors of apocolypse

Worthlessness

semantics || more worthless
a relationship gives meaning || additional or further
lagging to assess || less than immanent || less
than || historically reliable || comparative adjectives
measure indicators of potential || more worthless
employment || failed to answer || questionnaire
a cherry on top || to reflect not just a job || a false pretense
myself compared to others || a regulatory
framework || more worthless || depreciation
of the common || trading negatives
more || as in the phrase a more worthless person
to import || drawn definition || downturn logistics
I feel utterly || undefined || adrift voices
more worthless comparisons

1) the presence of a property

2) the silhouette of another

3) the presence of a certain property in one does not
   imply the presence of a related property in another

The Anatomist

You are a union of liquids and solids. The city layers over your skin, becomes your excess. You remain out of reach. You are bound by ligaments, moved by muscles. Call your feelings "complicity with chance." Knot your fingers, keep them still. You close your eyes when the light streams in at this angle. You return illegible after each attempt. You self-regulate. In all likelihood, you agree with the following description. You settle for less. You are reduced, by chemical analysis, to essential elements. Your borderline becomes overly familiar, constitutes a doorway passed as routine. You divide the objects under investigation into sections and subsections. You market yourself as a bargain. You sense the weight of your arms against the edge of the table, the book held open. Involuntary actions afflict your muscles with purpose as measurements replace bodies. You irritably reach after fact and reason. You are performing well from the outside. Every day, in every way, you adjust to cope with the weather. Reconnect with old friends as if you'd never left. You hold your twisted ankle. This, you are happy to discover, is a case of reversed metamorphosis. You abide uncertainty. You hold sway over public policy. You're a mess. You're a big fucking mess. You are a fibre of exceeding fineness, or several fibres bundled together, or a network of tissue, or an arrangement of tissue for a specific function. This is not a hospital room, nor a madhouse, though you feel that it could be either. You open into the pharynx, at its superior extremity, and communicate, by inferior opening, with the trachea. Through the window, you see a sign that reads, "You are, in following, yourself." You smack of falsehood. You can either have one or the other. Let tigers friendly riot in your blood. In the objects of your labour you discover yourself. You must be fun at parties. You were a good person and you will be missed. Refracting humours, or mediums, fill your interior globe. This poem is about you. How embarrassing for you. You go on. Make a list of your tasks. You plead guilty on the witness stand. You require nosological coding for causes of death. An outcome in which you dwell. You drive past your hometown, ignore the highway cut-offs. As you perceive the world around you, it's always cloudy. You aid in the intonation of the voice. By modification you understand the structure and manner of aggregation, not the precise form or magnitude, which indeed varies at every moment. The time taken in your performance of an idea replicates the time taken in your performance of muscular gestures. You blanch, hold a mirror to your mouth, wait for condensation to form on the glass. In shape you resemble a leaf of parsley. A growling dog recognizes its threat to your body. You distrust artificial building materials. Sitting in the doctor's chair you learn Latin. You understand the composition of the material under investigation. You shadow to cop personality. Assemble organs according to your plan or method. You recreate scenes, stage minutia of past experience, to maintain a physical connection. You ascend and evaporate, or pass off in the morning breeze. You play with the excesses that separate. In dissection you favour beasts whose nature approaches your own. You cancel out when formally calculated. Opening your eyes you bridge a binary. You must take an active role in your treatment. While queuing, you spell the word in your mind, picturing a black hole of vowels. You will decide for yourself, when the time comes, or you will depart undecided. You intervene between the interior and middle spongy bones. You run your nail along the seam of the pillowcase. You read and perceive a shifting collection of cells. You may be classified by etiology, pathogenesis, or symptom. Stuttering names in the phonebook, you convert a vocal knot to art. You arbitrarily check boxes on the claims form. You habituate your disease. You are an organ composed of distinct organs. The conceit of this alone makes you melancholy. You are the object of study here. Aren't you a sight for sore eyes. You will say: this is all very well but you describe only ephemeral organs, bodies, systems. Thank you investors. Thank you for cheering me up. Thank you for fighting alongside us. In the window seat you dare yourself to imagine plummeting through the air. You assume the principle, forgo component analysis. You patronize a vacuity of glass hallways, arcades of meandering desire. Atmospheric air, when you inspire it, consists of oxygen combined with nitrogen, but when you expire, the oxygen disappears. You look around and above every morning to observe if the mist falls or rises. You respirate to cool blood, to ease the muscles of the heart. You reorganize the objects to obscure the form. In triage you compare likeness and unlikeness — likeness the best sign, unlikeness the most dangerous. You perform an important office in the organization. You charm society by the ardour of your affections. Your membership entitles you to discounts on hotels, car rentals, and more. You reread books without remembering them. Your body contains no such space as cavity. If you were to burn a bone in a fire for fifteen minutes it would become white and brittle because the animal matter has been destroyed. You isolate readers in the lyric. Do not touch the spigot with your mouth or anything that has touched your mouth. Was it you, or you, or you. When you avoid eye contact you look up. Your hands wet with sweat. You produce capital. You might wander into the wilderness alone. Stretch yourself thin. Capital produces you. Marginalia skews your interpretation of the text. You play at mourning. You contract the diaphragm, create negative pressure. The reflection squints back at you. Animal motions of the organs of sense account for all of your theories and ideas. You bet you're fucked. You forget the combination, the composition. For melodious speaking or singing, you require atmospheric elasticity. You are not a thing so much as a way things happen. Anything you can do, you can do better. Immobility determines your diagnosis. You can open the door from the inside. You pay no attention to the words of others. As a collector you devise a new historical system among seemingly unrelated possessions. You offer only palliative comfort. You do not read the poem differently now. Your organs of sense, like moving muscles, are liable to become benumbed, or less sensible, from compression. Everything if you evaporate. Hands in pockets, you shuffle outside the apartment building, waiting for someone to unlock the door. You become a closed system. You know not what it is to leave the roof that shelters you. You short circuit. You feel nostalgia for the good old days. You must request a receipt before paying. You receive nerve signals from the sympathetic organs. You rewrite an anachronistic schema. You disbelieve the heart's slight mechanical impulse. Repeat your liquid routines. You, or someone like you. A collection of similar parts, many softer than your bones. It's your fault. You are a diversity of form and texture.

Of Matter Diverse and Confused. *Sect. 2.*

Personal Account. *Subsect. 1.*

Stayed the course because it sounded universal. As animal spirits
follow predictable motions, parties remote move our limbs
from their place.

Unprepared armaments. Fantasies coerce invalids to walk on planks
set high, and from such height to describe the ground below, the wind
against a body.

Spend feel like a self. Stare at the wall and dwell between confines
of sense and reason. Love mourning, the first. Built
calamities.

Painful wakings require particular treatment beyond declamatory praises
of the physical specimen. Just below the surface. Now explain this vacancy
as a ship of fools.

So the event of being reasserts itself in the question. Rebels nervy
in the domestic body. As mariners to sea stow necessities to resist a tempest
we furnish ourselves with philosophical examples.

Cause Effect. *Subsect. 2.*

Some signs remain secret, some manifest, some in the body, some
in the mind, and diversely. Continues to night. Avert sensitive choirs
that grab by turns of logic.

Species directly given to imagination project threats. Watery and terrestrial
though burnt and about to fall for the ruse. Predatory instincts in thickets
of uneven landscape.

Replicate a thwarted return. Twin-born inseparable companions
swap a fluid dialogue. The specific distinction in these limbs: their
consensus.

Like the wild boar a riotous pulse. Now nearer, now farther off, together,
asunder. One may delight in faction, though often its strong conceit
punishes wits.

Happy is the city that in times of peace dreams of war. A painting
captivates cheerlessly. More or less deep impressions that fashion
a rigid furniture.

Though altitude and atmosphere do agitate impersonally, every society,
corporation, and family is full of some such stimuli. Emulations that shadow
a captive envy.

Pine Away. *Subsect. 3.*

Are they solitary for pleasure, one asks, or for pain. Yet rather
for fear. Ourselves minus reason and affectivity. Restless minds cannot
sleep for fix on the object of delirium.

Heavy hearts begin to sigh. Insatiable desires imagined as replies
to unknown provocations. Questions jeer content. Prone to heat
and easily taken.

Activity indicates no change. Somnolent affects sketch impressions, pressed
expressions and a riotous pulse. What you name are the hallucinatory
confluences of clean research.

Plot now gone, he fancies the clocks reset. The safest course a blind eye,
a deaf ear. Market chatter continues. When matter is diverse and confused
how else could the mind be.

With a digression of air a wing flits inward. There, error clans another.
Repetition of a fundamental pose. Our fluids move. We've a palliative
impulse, a patient's time.

Spreading Sheets

Of the Stratus

It is the lowest of Clouds since its inferior surface commonly rests on the earth or water.

This is properly the cloud of night; the time of its first appearance being about sun-set. It comprehends all those creeping Mists which in calm evenings ascend in spreading sheets (like an inundation) from the bottom of valleys and the surface of lakes, rivers, and other pieces of water to cover the surrounding country.

—Luke Howard, *Essay on the Modification of Clouds*

Report:

what is this fog?

Everything if I evaporate. Wipe condensation from the bathroom mirror, stare to eyes as sky outside shifts. Currently in the preconstruction phase. Sun breaks in the west. I waited for hours, but no flights arrived. Scanning the crowd, searching for anything familiar.

3 hours ago

patches dissipate   by morning

commute dawn   becomes

patchy Vancouver over the last

couple of days

Motorists drive with extra caution. System-wide delays. Overheard conversations perceived as violent in the intensity of the speakers' descriptions of others. Eyes begin to water from the effort of sight. Information about entrance restrictions, health and security advisories.

7 hours ago   Oct 12

morning this weekend

As ridiculous as longing for another person. Despite the influx of supply, rental rates remain strong. Braced for balance, burnt off with the morning sun. How does I constitute a need in my mind, shape thought's lack. Downward revisions.

develop expectations   developing

weather on Sunday   then mostly dense

Oct 6   swirl

lingering

Strangers discuss weather over breakfast and arrive home before dark. Here, where strandlines run parallel with the ocean, chart lines of debris.

visibility issues   10 minutes ago

horizontally layer flat   hazy, featureless

Report:

advisory sun to shine

Sep 24   before midnight

patches developing

Minutes of inertia. Recordings, imaginings all affected by the ebb. For I am a relatively sophisticated market participant. Blame is measuring the length of one's arms.

27 minutes ago

what is this fog?

Follow line past end of outstretched fingers. Continue to measure until hitting an obstruction. A wall, a crowd, a strong wind.

drivers early

blanketed roads

oft-repeated expect

Site information and feedback. Use market-adjusted returns, and nobody looks back. Passenger experience prioritized. I cannot see the object of my mourning.

43

sports, weather   through

rapid movement

Gravity presses in on both the room and its occupants. Equity investors also affected by climate conditions. The evaporation of faces. Reread books, places previously occupied. Becoming tired of the spectacle, the crowd talks amongst themselves about the unseasonable chill.

prevailing winds

observed at: Vancouver Int'l Airport

Speaking of wellness. Discount rates. Impressions left on others' minds vary little. Clothes, habits, ruins, projected completion dates.

sun break

apart night   10 hours ago

Report:

pressure

Tomorrow is a workday, so tonight I will go to bed early. For your convenience: a listings of 'bad' neighbourhoods.

so dense

covering metro

up to 25°C

tapering encounters

Arm braced against the door as if for balance. Financial forecast, rising projections. Idling, still in the car, the need to relocate binds passengers to the machine.

cloaking

stuck-on-repeat

what is this fog?

Of the animals seen today, only the crows' daily migration strikes the eye as symbolic. A rezoning in progress. Everything is on sale except for waterproof outerwear.

hovering mainland

updated: a few minutes ago

low   pressure zones

Crowd exiting bus passes their reflection in police car windows.

mists

daytime low

A fun experiment: compare stock exchanges at varying latitudes. Did the forecast say humanity or humidity?

midst

cancelled dense

Report:

visibility

Reports thin to sparse, crackle words between stations. Must be cloud cover and an insufficient belief in fate.

shrouded

Workers mistake windows for grey painted canvases.

power outages

Abnormal returns in fall due to an increased discount rate. Sleep deprived disguised as busy. Re: room for rent.

regardless

road conditions

Presale sales of the world's first fully trans-
formable homes. Weather conditions fluctuate
on two axes.

and

Hard to get up. A collection of symptoms.
Fingers' bored pace across keyboard.

national

what is this fog?

The open magazine advises regular exercise and
sleep. Recession indicators detailed by persons
of credit.

Sep 6

likely

Never answer the question 'how are you' with a
description of mood or physical state.

primary effects

Pull wet hands across curtains, dark lines fade
to fingers' impressions. Something built up,
something posed.

surround

                              offshore

Report:

and

Coastline traces a current mood.

precipitation:

Sodden paper moulds to sidewalk. The dialectics of interior and exterior reduce experience to passport.

50%

swerve

In bed for days at a time, turning dictionary pages. Arrange proof

6:15AM

chronologically before announcing the presence of a trend.

fog

Sound buying decisions

10°C

with accurate
information. Tell me about the unreliability of
self-diagnosing.

pressure

less

Rooms built in the streets reverse a false
distinction. Seasons purely exogenous, thus data
remains accurate despite fluctuations. Neutral

clear

returns. Horizon and its
algorithm.

droplets

8°C

Routines test forgery as a method for coping
with absence.

continue

patchy

Public acts of wasting away.

what is this fog?

Crystal Healing

observe that no description of life applies to these

in press forces composite suppressed lithium
deposit traces cause nausea salt projected mine
lifespan halfway healed
point out metaphysical properties
practitioners sign corruptive impact
benefit settlement
mineral side effect lists

yield by folding to lateral pressure, flow instead of breaking

shift stubborn claims
augment regimens
reported revenue bends discourse lived
sites span jewelry idle steamroller
withdrawn to disorder
crush risk brush profits pharmacological
landmass statistics

symmetry replicated in the minutest detail

ulcerous production factory setting
withdrawn values tax
bracket clumsy proposals natural sites mineral
relief systemic affects sustain
runoff ordered invoices prescriptive slicks insurance
chakra left half untapped
life taught tensions slip
convenient studies after stone cold facts
price refracted inventory

any fractures healed at once by the pressing of grain to grain

net loss resonates calming gross alternative
medicine bedrocks geoeconomic manias
approximate sources calculate energy
embodied leaky tap calculations spirit
fractious investors
test cathartic anxieties

forever imperceptible, inevitable growth

scatter generative
geologic risk
diamonds workforce
crystallized scatterbrain
haptic tests
flail edges
consolidate maps
fluctuate prisms
precious electric
drip habits
press anxious
penetrate nervous
system crack
bejeweled risk
unfit margin
cornered organic
gestures static
modeled outcomes
fevered doctors
 advise alternative
quick fixes

murkier streams convey substance, the strongest

tricks scrap bodies proximate
abandon tax tactics compress
mental chatter feedback blurs migraine
third quarter growth
trinket discussion tracks cheap dosage decrease
clinical studies sticks stone thick skin practice
forest contract adverse effect
list tract pendants
suppress painful regimes
manage comment section like
crystal necklace
status to board access historic presence
crass plastic spans psychic evacuate

they that grow more rapidly after being broken

dysphoric quartz
pictures original measurement device
diamond tipped drills
sunlit project summary set reports
prism victims of untapped poetic twitch
takes root awaits divided spectrum related
relief efforts effect
disaffected treatment
rewires switch tricks pharmacy
sleight of hand cracks skin
of onstage hacks
brokered etymology fixed in resin
patient promotes profit overdose
frantic craft
once daily scripts alternate records

Of Matter Diverse and Confused. *Sect. 3.*

Immedicable Minds. *Subsect. 1.*

As an oar in water refracted seems bigger, bent double we saw
two suns. Concerning the patient, we must counterfeit confidence,
succumb to libelled bindings.

All succeeding ages will subscribe. Notwithstanding they know
such miseries. They suffer themselves. Hunger is not ambitious, though
wasted with desire.

Fit poverty played out in a breath. Eyes against a tented spectacle.
The driver's hum, the boy's sick ballad. Such tunes for timid children.
We purgers arm in arm.

The latest scandal came close to the truth. Mimic the mimicking
voices of all birds. Embroidered waterways tangle, succumb to commerce.
Ships and their mad denizens.

A brittle world floating on the sea. Fabric wrapped tight against limbs
restricts gesture. Barbaric scholars stand by. The voyage's error delivers
garments threadbare.

Listless Fibres. *Subsect. 2.*

The common unrest, a mind inattentive, unsettled in a vast
confusion of vows, wishes, edicts, petitions, lawsuits, pleas,
laws, proclamations, complaints, grievances

set loose in absent recreation in new books every day, pamphlets,
stories, whole catalogues of volumes, miscellanies of like paradoxes,
unlike opinions, schisms, heresies

bound within and without in controversies of philosophy, religion, lapsed
tidings of weddings, jubilees, embassies, tournaments, failures
to articulate

those mutual triumphs, revels, sports, treasons, cheats, robberies,
villainies, funerals, burials, deaths, an ambitious reaching within
the vacillating stream of discoveries, expeditions

now comical, then tragical matters of attention lapsed in wretched parody
of new lords and officers, great men deposed, fresh honours conferred,
the majesty and misery of the world

bound hemispheric in a figure of peevish devotion to the roamings of jollity,
pride, perplexities and cares, simplicity and villainy, in one public body
all mutually mixed offerings.

Commit Folly. *Subsect. 3.*

Rain falls on both sides of the boundary, soaks down through layers
to fill a hidden well. That feral sadness tortures the soul, speaks
of the world to come.

Is it normal to feel disquiet, to not freely move, to quake and scowl.
The sentimental necessity of writing, the waste of indulging
other creatures.

Say there's no beginning waiting. That all physicians do enforce
nature with hired acclimations. Market stalls mete with unconvincing
conceits.

No precedent for diagnosing recovery. The heart and the mind
do mutually misaffect one another. Our revenues otherwise employed
to coax an addiction.

All ages enforce order based on anteriority. A living source, so living,
so constant. Our present lack incomprehensible. Coercions drawn
in procedure, numbers mounting.

Augers maintain that in such empty gestures love reigns. Gardens
weather each winter, cedars and black bark. To exert oneself among
annals distracts from seasonal conditions.

What We Call Vacuity

as a single letter common among many words
                    inserted
those who deem such leaks accidents, sources found
                    neither material nor effective
they say: liquid to sea (nature craves no
                    artifice, no luxury (no food chain of regret

touch diffused over skin, a moderate depression
of voice   alerts in your area: ammonia, hazmat, mercury
moves by virtue of few   withdrawn (added few

vast torrent of negation   whether chance or force
                    credits tongues through such thick wells

eyes cannot view objects manifest
                    thus   respirate the solid operation

diesel bridges to river   90L   262kg   3600gal
113L   3x   100x   32kg   second flow a boundary

subtle films   layer to volume
deposits red or black (iron or manganese

substance stuck to throat   infinite attributes
restore connection between former (latter
                            translated 'without feeling'

protest memory, reference   sliding groundwater
interrogates superficialities and gradations of type

title smears continue toward interior pages
eye (skin irritation, immunosuppression, keep tight

remove innermost values first   relieve them

bodies consume lands (legions, such artillerymen all
intercalculations

                        departed limits shore a dawning

compare the wreck of vessels, barrels' splintered path
from walkways' overpass   visible objects scatter

remediation trains (laden (erode the skirting lens

faults unpardonable (as portioned to nature
                in number the density of utility

right principles require perpetual increase
subtractive terms weigh   (bounds in the final curve

subtle luxury prepares flowers, gaudy
        gasses   drawn up by industrious root

as sounds through well closed rooms affect
        bones (matter downward tends

could such coalition, such atoms infer
        decipherability in a nervous system's thicket

mere branches shoot the tenable motion
        reroute (or plant discretionary, porous

vapour pressed to corpus clouds a window
            corrosives through breach reports

called seeds or   particles: actions
themselves forget (stowed offshore, anchored

here hazel bent to tide   yet beasts refused
birds fled all wings away (animals complete

assured stable conditions, limited risk assessment
forehead leant against border   wave's soft edge

why make such bodies (why labour at all

queries and doubts in plastic earth (particulate matter
loiters among shored winds

suppose a fence to encompass, compress, prevent
erosion

tearing wood to grain one may endeavour
to uncover the basal matters

tracks only voided
ether (which weather borne such rapid lightness

limbs trail shoreline,　　　trail breadcrumbs
　　　　to ocean (form two quantities from one equation

figures translated before the bracket affect those enclosed

so collate the dyed fractures
　　　　place the decimal at the (wingspan

remember zero through thermometer glass
ammonia among the spray (establish moisture in thought

ships through night (jettisoned letters of false receptors

what bird presumes to steer   liquid sky (drifts
                    rudderless down influent lines

All We Ever Wanted Was Everything

Cellular as a stance. A move to motion. Or
otherwise delineated standard, written out.
This list of examples supports a similar
claim. Still, gesticulate and wait. It has always
been us and them, waiting to get to
the front. Awaiting a disaster of timepieces.
Hands in pockets. Phone in pocket. Keys
in pocket. To get to the front navigate
the passage as it's narrated. Rerun.
The return binds industry, numbers
quantity. Pre-packaged, pre-read. No one
called next. Lines repeat unnoticed.
A stance again, another. Equally isolated
oversights bind viewer recognition. This
is a theory of high art.

Maps still hold a stilled world. Struggle
through work to coffee break.
Indeterminate, a we allows together
to hold. Face to back of head.
Plots course against felt lines.
Fabric depends upon a belief of sorts.
Each interleaved bind an ignored
remark. An insufficient awareness
of the limits of chance. Tickets
serve as proxy, flammable.
Burnt on unplugged monitors. Lean
on context, assume an absence.
Important words printed in bold.
Animals roam the aisles. Fill in
the blanks. A motion mocked.
Best before dates stamped around
here somewhere. I've been here
before haven't I?

Excuse me, I had planned to stumble
over another body. Not your
body. As casual as industry gets.
When a situation outlives the
potential for honesty. Recedes
to background noise, becomes
imperceptible. You were an innocent
bystander. Display case rolls back
into the entranceway when store
is closed. Calling it in today. I've
spoken too loudly, given something
away too early. Among daily specials
apologizing for commitment.
Movement may only be calculated
as memory. Tinned radio silent
until noticed, then unbearable.
With faces filed singly, snaking
asemic patterns. A scene ensues.
To vacation among atmospheric
noises. Anyone in the administration
would recognize value. Work to find
the pure form of this arrangement.

Face registers little. Repetition
reroutes thinking. All I ever wanted
was everything. The difference
between saying something and
saying something to someone.
Like a too-loud laugh that hangs
awkwardly above a conversation.
People use this as an excuse.
I'm ignoring you to see if you'll make
an effort. They display their boredom
as status symbol, but they're at
the front of the theatre. This noise
everywhere, its periphery nowhere.
The exchange draws attention. Need
caffeine to get through the day.
Seats arranged so as to preclude
a proper view of the performance.
Feedback encouraged. Discomfort
may or may not constitute this
performance. A gap. A path to otherwise
maneuver. Aware of hungry bodies.

Of Matter Diverse and Confused. *Sect. 4.*

Fabric Suffers. *Subsect. 1.*

If pressed, we'd describe ourselves as absent. Where sleep binds
listless fibres and nerves perceive any tensile quality. We know not how
many cities bear this record, tactics of subversion.

Discussion turns to quarantine of physicians ashamed to admit personal
disease. Exquisite movement of sense within organs. Buildings tremble,
and citizens fear the end of the world.

This raging madness. Protests and swears. Heaven's tempests dissuade
maladjusted meat. Though still waters run deep standing lakes
stagnate quickly.

The fault of the form, a whole temperature. A body reckons these signs
a stupefied grief. As hounds pursue a false train never perceive themselves
at fault.

Frequent battles and the perpetual memorial. Begun in folly, continued
to crime, and ended in crisis. Utopian parity desired rather than
effected.

Subtle lineaments slice breath through city corridors. Spilt liquids drift
by density among the organs. So often they study to misuse each other, wits
disquiet.

Corollary Questions. *Subsect. 2.*

Are you a mixture of hot and cold. Are you nauseous with uncomfortable
fullness. What enemy is this. How many such spirits does it contain. And
what further proofs of misaffection needed.

Do you suffer an overflowing of thought, a constant anxiety, a constant
staring at only one thing. Does your anatomy afford the mobile
desires of multiple tongues.

Do you opine your skull to be glass. Who is not vulnerable amid
planetary conjunction, moved in foul weather, dull and heavy
in such tempestuous seasons.

Do you have fumes rising from your spleen. What will not a fearful
mortal conceive in dark. What violent motions. What distempers
rise from limited sense.

Have you mouthed ornate syllables recently. Have words thrown
sand in eyes, provoked grief, labour, care, pale sickness, melancholia,
fear, poverty, hungers that cry without relief.

Particular Subjects. *Subsect. 3.*

The temperature of the body overthrown. Left impulses, memory.
Inability being a common infirmity. Like kingdoms under such heads
bodies groan.

Mock folly, mock one another. As a murmur unprofitable. Such
an economy of motion. Bankrupt neighbours. Actors intrude
on the common ground.

One purchases, another breaks. Diverse medics beckon. And those
who live inland desire islands. These small neglects worn
as bejeweled cloaks.

Acknowledge proximity. For each action, an equal and inverse
mania. The theatre of minor aches and pains mocks
sovereign ailments.

No money but mercurial. By moving, the body's outwardly carried, yet
inwardly moved also. Felt pressure and flashing vision before the barricades.
Exhale maligned vapours.

Proceeds from organic parts. Temperature regulates limbs. Touch,
the final sense and most ignoble. Their organs, their objects. Injuries
to displace a heavy appetite.

Uncertainty Measures

Incalculable. Daily tasks

                        Laugh strains pitch, hangs overhead

Seen in the desire for fortune in the thick of illness

   Debt adages foreign currency. Tastes overdraft translation

On a scale of 1 to 10

                     Light bulb incorporates. "Burnt-out"

Speaking of cliffs   Stats bolster speculation

Our disclosure policy:

      Borderline cases that being and non-being become

                             Stilled tense

                           Air tight to lungs

Of number   Stairs impress rib-like
Retrenchment demand articulates   Etches breath

Regulate intake. From slump to stand-still

"We suffer now from an attack of economic pessimism"
The best antidote is a good night's rest

That's my problem: I'm too literal.   Reuptake

          Leftover. Underwritten outpatient rooms
          Where implausible methods soften muscle
                    Loose thread at curtain's edge

Snagged intent, progress weaves accordingly
                              Entangle dust, collect hair

Reckless spending luxuriates differentiating potential
            1 2 3 4 5 6 7 8 9 10

                    Standing in the field, thoughts reroute
                                        Opt to return

Customer service adjusts to the needs and personality
Of the guest   "Hear what you have to say"

Orders filled from stockpiles

               Voice reinforces a textured ceiling

               Traps covered with dead leaves

                  Dreamt broken bone

"The good days are over

Lay back and let capital take its course"

Speculate on current climates.

               Driving conditions

Estranged agreement. Synaptic layers reword connective

Delayed too long without consolidation

            A difference of attention begins to make itself felt

Veins open into accounts, investment

Posit a mind operating within a body.

Easy-speak for "business-cycle"

Whispers twined through cords. Receiver touches floor

Wall measurements trace time to excess

Moved to impress fingers to window glass

Observe the arrangement of living matter

Oak leaves shadow the lawn

Survival tips?
Two words:

New incomes

Pre-existing conditions

|| bruised sky || fed structure || fold evenly || after getting ||
kept it || while lying || felt childish || nerve energy || empty
patterns ||

Pre-existing conditions

First word
Second word

Five things to hold on to:

Years of austerity climate and a tough road

Live up to employment

Editorialize desired windfall

Slow leak above stairs

Sodden layers leaf off

(Y / N)

Remainders of soaked strata

(Y / N)

(Y / N)

(Y / N)

(Y / N)

Hard times don't happen overnight

Cry for help

Hot migraines enact a contoured awareness

Report findings of an extensive survey and ask for input

Whereas habits require names

Feedback. Please provide your feedback here:

Exercises patience, rejects meals, bides time

Lawn braces to brick, closes in

Midday sun pulled taut through branches

Seasonal markup

Here

Daylight savings increases productivity
Borrowed stock phrases   Dishes and stacked ephemera

Choose symptom(s)

Strained muscles live through expression
                    Recession is over, but   Pacing with phone in hand

            Remember, this is part of the regular rhythm
Speech stimulus
                    Your choices

Budget calculated in the margin
                            Rearrange furniture to distract
                Possible condition   Note lines'
                                                Overlap

Return Policy

Credit happiness to predictability.
A year or two becomes desire to rebuild.

This dangerous impulse, a kind of desertion.
So go home, try to be good.

Face to unrecognizable face. Note creases
on forehead, the open mouth beginning to speak.

The pressure of occurrence interrupts a response.
Fingerprints inked on concrete revisions.

Cups of cold coffee, an unused spoon.
Such objects keep us together, apart together.

Proper name embodies an interpretive delay. Never
cured by repetition—a drawn-out line.

The actors affect a critical attitude, draw themselves
against the darkness of unlit corners.

Subtle skin begins to peel. Recall security pressed
to sense. Lost and found bins everywhere.

When hearing similar sentiments spelled
differently brokers nostalgia.

Triggers continue to disrupt temporal experience.
So continue farther afield.

As far as the eye can see the eye overlooks.
I left before the questions, cut losses in the uproar.

The gracious humour of ellipsis. Head tilts
to wind while muscles twitch beneath skin.

The disguises were worst. How they corresponded
to your features. Dried runnels describe

a narrow route to the source. Take a break.
Drink water. Long for obscure fashions.

Imbalanced notebook pages. Tried to speak.
An emotionless language declined.

Darting eyes seek reassurance of a common
frenzy. Unopened letters in doorway.

Reference passes through writing. In the dream
the interlocutor refused, moved a glass

from the edge of the table. An experiment
in silence. I don't lose sleep over it. Self-help

is just how capitalism feels. So trust unwinds
binds limbs to cities, vacancies to furniture.

Proximity counterfeits acquaintance. Today,
a note. Less than a letter, a single sentence.

Projectors pitch lit fabrics. Pull knees
to chest, wrap arms to hold in place.

Simply greeted, no exchange. Voices matched
to digital gestures.

Albums of discarded possessions. Such entities
spoken. Wingtips obliterate mountaintops

from this seat's perspective. Such
is the way with wild creatures, short-lived.

Nails bit to blood. Creased
histories burn verso's brief shade.

I knew the rules from the outset, but forgot
the implications. Motion discloses coarse

approximations of an instinct. The sky clears
and bodies return to tracing soft prints.

Continues to disrupt impartial measurement.
Like capital expresses a nervous system

deprived of touch. Personal documents filed
among pressed leaves, receipts. Remote voices

screen a distance splayed as light. Gravity among
overlaid possessions. Not a break, an evacuation.

Of Matter Diverse and Confused. *Sect. 5.*

Systematic Arrangements. *Subsect. 1.*

Exquisite sense. This labyrinth of accidental causes. Gently brings sensation as a siren to the irrevocable gulf. Harsh departure and outward animal motions.

From causes operating on the bodily frame. Reject excessive mobility, drink water to manage moisture. Judgments scaled against minerals inflexible to the skin.

All ailments rise as fountains from a dilated heart. Peripatetic faculty of three requisite parts: that which moves, by which it moves, and that which is moved.

Eyes weigh the common catastrophe against the trade. Diverse, all tempered and mingled containers. Scratch tough hide, expose tendons stretched beneath the spoken form.

But we conclude: the pit of symptoms disrupts our model. Though we sense a state of disrupted faculty in excessive labour of mind, fanaticism, zeal, revolutions, etc. As ships run ashore in hunger, we misaffect.

Review

This book is depressing.

God, this book is depressing.

Man, this book is depressing.

Overall this book is depressing.

In a way this book is depressing.

Answer: this book is depressing.

Um, yeah, this book is depressing.

Damn, but this book is depressing.

The mood of this book is depressing.

I'm depressed, this book is depressing.

This book is depressing as hell, though.

Update: this book is depressing as fuck.

This book is depressing, with a capital D.

Oh my goodness, this book is depressing.

This book is depressing in a cathartic way.

Some have said that this book is depressing.

This book is depressing all the way through.

Overall, this book is depressing in its reality.

This book is depressing, funny yet depressing.

This book is depressing for a fluffy beach read.

For some reason, this book is depressing to me.

This book is depressing as fuck but it's worth it.

Do you think this book is depressing or hopeful?

Warning: This book is depressing, cruel and sad.

My life is depressing and this book is depressing.

This book is depressing and intentionally boring.

This book is depressing because it is so persuasive.

This book is depressing to someone of my age (70).

I can't tell if this book is depressing or if I'm just sad.

I think this book is depressing yet strangely uplifting.

This book is depressing me, but I just can't put it
down.

The reason this book is depressing is from page 1 to
200.

Admittedly, reading this book is depressing as all get
out.

I can't decide whether this book is depressing or
hilarious.

Why raise the question of whether this book is

depressing?

This book is depressing and poorly written and
researched.

I was told this book is depressing and I wasn't sure
why at first.

This book is depressing, with not many bright spots in
between.

This book is depressing, horrifying, disgusting and
heartbreaking.

This whole beginning of this book is depressing the
shit out of me.

Please don't let me talk you into believing that this
book is depressing.

Also the readers who said this book is depressing are
quite funny to me.

This book is depressing me because everyone's lives
suck in this book.

If you are afraid that this book is depressing, then I
can ease your mind.

I could spend several paragraphs discussing how this
book is depressing.

About 80% of this book is depressing to any
thoughtful or caring person.

This book is depressing, right up until it turns
incredibly sappy and sweet.

Yes this book is depressing because the ending does
not really satisfy you.

This book is depressing depressing depressing and not
visually interesting.

Yes, this book is depressing, but in that rare beautiful
way some things can be.

Depending on your mood, this book is depressing,
frightening and/or hilarious.

This book is depressing, but somewhat gives you a
sense of adventure and love.

From my opening statement you might think this
book is depressing, but it is not!

Dear Reader, curl up with a bottle of wine and tissues,
cuz this book is depressing.

Based on what I've said above, you might get the
impression this book is depressing.

Although this book is depressing to read at times, it

also seems realistic and practical.

The history described in this book is depressing, but
the present is somewhat brighter.

I mean this book is depressing enough without a
person keeling over every two pages.

I find it depressing my father thinks "This book is
depressing" is a criticism of a book.

Frankly, much of this book is depressing — a happy
ending is an absolute impossibility.

To summarize, this book is depressing, wayward,
inconclusive and completely brilliant.

The humour in part one and part two is kind of hard
to find since this book is depressing.

Make no mistake, this book is depressing, but it sends
a message that no one should miss.

If I were to give in to my first impression, I would have
to say that, above all, this book is depressing.

I know, some people will still be worried that this
book is depressing, simply because of the subject
matter.

This book is depressing; I couldn't get to sleep fully

because I kept thinking about it, how lame is that?

This book is depressing and should only be read by eyes who are forced to read it unless you like depressing books.

Reading through this book is depressing; it is all so logical, so calmly explained — yet utterly useless when you think about it.

If you are looking for a comedy or happy story, I would suggest reading something else because this book is depressing and sad.

Although this book is depressing and does not have the usual happy ending, I would advise reading this book, especially for those who write.

In part this book is depressing, as many of the lives I discovered within the covers are humourless and well a little bit disappointing, but hey I guess that's life.

This book is depressing; if you're looking for a feel-good book in which everything turns out to be super and everybody gets puppies, you'll be sorely disappointed.

This book is depressing as heck, I was in a complete funk for about a day after I read it, to the point where I had to watch a cute, fluffy movie to get over said funk.

I know, for many, this book is depressing or difficult to make sense of and seems to portray a sense of hopelessness, but I think it is a book written to show us the futility of things.

I agree that this book is depressing and some readers may not enjoy reading something this authentic and real, but I also believe that it is important for readers to get a different perspective on life.

One question that a lot of people asked me was whether this book is "depressing," which I think is an appropriate question since the story is about a college student with depression; however, upon finishing the book, I can't help but think how optimistic it made me feel after reading it.

This book is depressing and the weather isn't helping but luckily someone has ripped out the last few pages which has cheered me up seriously if you're

a writer give us a glimpse of hope here and there
and we'll keep reading what I'm saying is you know
when you read a depressing book and it has a
depressing ending and you become depressed yeah
that's basically me right now.

I write of melancholy, by being busy to avoid melancholy.
—Robert Burton

Notes

"Of Matter Diverse and Confused" writes with and through the vocabulary and diction of Robert Burton's *Anatomy of Melancholy*, as well as a number of other seventeenth- and eighteenth-century indexes and nosologies, including François Boissier de Sauvages's *Nosologie Méthodique* and William Cullen's *Synopsis Nosologiae Methodicae*.

The titles and some language found in "Depression Inventory" derive from the Beck's Depression Inventory, a standard diagnostic survey.

Many sentences in "The Anatomist" were composed by inserting the pronoun "you" in place of the names of organs in pre-twentieth-century medical texts.

"Spreading Sheets" is of and for Vancouver. Greyed text derives from a daily practice of transcribing weather report descriptions of fog in Vancouver over the course of about two months during the fall of 2013.

"Crystal Healing" writes with and through online advertisements for crystals sold to relieve anxiety and depression, pharmaceutical information about lithium and SSRIs, and reports of the environmental and social impact of Northern Ontario diamond mining.

"What We Call Vacuity" is for Sarnia, Ontario, and the communities surrounding the Chemical Valley, especially the Aamjiwnaang First Nation, who experience ongoing environmental racism (see: https://aamjiwnaangsolidarity.com/). The poem employs some vocabulary from early translations of Lucretius's *De Rerum Natura*, as well as reports of spills, leaks, and air pollutants in the Chemical Valley region and the St. Clair River. The title derives from the only parenthetical phrase in R. E. Latham's 1951 translation of *De Rerum Natura*.

"All We Ever Wanted Was Everything" borrows its title from the Bauhaus song of the same name.

Several lines in "Return Policy" are rewritten phrases from Jacques Derrida's *The Work of Mourning*.

"Review" transcribes and arranges sentences mined from Google results for the phrase "this book is depressing." The poem became the basis for the @Un_Review twitter bot, which was programmed to retweet any tweet in which the phrase "this book is depressing" appeared. The twitter bot created a live-updating poem that ran for about half of a year until it crashed in 2015.

Acknowledgements

Earlier versions of some of these poems appeared in *Acta Victoriana*, *Canadian Literature, COUGH, Dreamland, Eleven Eleven, fillingStation, The Hart House Review, Lemon Hound, Matrix, Poetry Is Dead, The Puritan, Rusty Toque*, and *Touch the Donkey*, as well as the anthologies *Avant Canada: More Useful Knowledge* (No Press, 2014) and *DIS_appointment* (Swimmers Group, 2016). My gratitude to the editors of these publications.

An early version of "Listless Fibres" was published in the chapbook anthology *EMBLAM* as "Survey," which was written in response to the musical composition titled "Plunge into the Gulf" by J. Zumpano.

Lines from "Spreading Sheets" appeared in the video poem "Vancouver Dispersed," created by Kevin Spenst and screened at the 2015 Visible Verse Festival in Vancouver.

Larger sections of *If Pressed* were published as chapbooks titled *I can't tell if this book is depressing or if I'm just sad* (No. Press, 2016), *This Book Is Depressing* (TMCBP, 2014), and *Conditional* (JackPine, 2014).

For advice, support, conversation, and/or care in the many stages of this project, thank you (in no particular order) to: Roy Miki, Carla Harryman, Oliver Cusimano, David Peter Clark, Jonathan Pappo, Anahita Jamali Rad, The UBC English Department, Laura and David Singleton, Phinder Dulai, Glenn Deer, Candace Couse, The Book Keeper, Chuckers, Joe Abel, Claire Potter, The Banff Centre's In(ter)ventions Studio and Steven Ross Smith, Elee Kralji Gardiner, derek beaulieu, The Paper Hound Bookshop, Julia Polyck O'Neill, Karen da Silva, Gregory Betts, Kevin Spenst, and the many others I've forgotten to mention.

Thank you to Erín Moure, Jordan Abel, and Ann Cvetkovich for kind words and thoughtful readings of this book.

Thank you to my editor, angela rawlings, whose care and attention drew together many loose threads of these poems.

Thank you to Jay, Hazel, and the BookThug family for their tireless support and confidence in this project.

Thank you always to Virginia Allan and Holly McEwan.

Andrew McEwan is the author of *repeater* (a finalist for the 2013 Gerald Lampert Memorial Award) and numerous chapbooks, including *Conditional* and *Can't tell if this book is depressing or if I'm just sad.* Originally from Bright's Grove, Ontario, he now lives in St. Catharines.

Colophon

Manufactured as the
first edition of *If Pressed*
in the fall of 2017 by BookThug

Distributed in Canada by
The Literary Press Group
lpg.ca

Distributed in the US by
Small Press Distribution
spdbooks.org

Shop online at
bookthug.ca

BOOK
PRODUCTION
WAR ECONOMY
STANDARD

Edited for the press by angela rawlings
Type + design by Jay Millar